# The Fire Mountains

## The story of the Cascade Volcanoes

Text by Beverly Magley
Illustrations by DD Dowden

## Dedication

For A.O.
. . . and all the mountains yet to climb

Copyright © 1990
by Falcon Press Publishing Co., Inc.,
Billings and Helena, Montana.

Illustrations by DD Dowden.

Design, typesetting, and other prepress work by Falcon Press, Helena, Montana. Printed in Singapore.

Library of Congress Number 88-83884
ISBN 0-937959-57-X

# CONTENTS

*We may think volcanoes destructive*
*With magma and gases eruptive*
*But lava and ash*
*Spit out with a crash*
*Is earth's way of being constructive*

The earth underfoot rumbled and trees swayed on the upper slopes of the volcano. Very slowly, a bulge grew near the summit, causing rocks and dirt to clatter downhill. Scientists were curious and excited. They monitored the volcano and watched their instruments as activity deep inside the volcano grew more intense.

KABOOM!!!

The blast was heard for hundreds of miles as pressure from below exploded out the top of the volcano. Steam rocketed skyward while gas-filled rock and ash erupted into the air. Lava gushed out of the summit crater and streamed down the mountainside. Glaciers melted by the intense heat roared down, carrying whole forests in the floods.

The sleeping volcano had awakened with a roar.

# WHAT IS A VOLCANO?

Our ancestors often made up stories about the mountains they saw every day. Native Americans believed the volcanoes were gods who sometimes grew angry and hurled molten rock and debris at each other. Ancient Romans thought the blacksmith of the gods lived on the island of Vulcan and the smoking volcano was the chimney of the blacksmith's giant forge. We get the name "volcano" from this island. In the early 1700s, a Frenchman argued that huge blobs of oil and fat were piled high underground from the animals and fishes that died during the great biblical flood. He thought volcanoes were those mountains of fat on fire, and predicted that eventually the whole globe would be consumed in a great, greasy, spattering ball of fire.

Today our understanding of volcanoes is more scientific, but we still have a lot to learn. Next year geologists may think of entirely new explanations for how volcanoes are formed, quite different from today's understanding. Maybe you will become a geologist with new ideas about volcanoes.

The word "volcano" can mean two things. A volcano can be an opening in the earth's crust through which hot materials such as gas, steam, and molten rock, or magma, get pushed out. Usually, though, "volcano" means the hill or mountain formed by the piles that were thrown out by this activity. Many geologists believe that everything around us—our water, our atmosphere, and our land—came from volcanoes which ejected gases, minerals, and solid materials onto the crust over hundreds of millions of years. So volcanoes aren't the destructive objects they seem. We may owe our lives to them!

An erupting volcano can blow a whole mountain to bits, leaving a crater, or hole, where land used to be. Crater Lake in Oregon is an example of this kind of volcano. A volcano may release steam, gases, ash, and lava. Lava Beds National Monument shows the many different kinds of lava that can erupt from a single volcano. Lava is magma that has reached the earth's surface.

If a volcano erupts over and over, the lava and ash build up in a pile around the hole, or vent, and form a mountain. Each eruption adds more layers to the mountain. Volcanoes formed in this way are called composite, or stratovolcanoes. Most Cascade volcanoes are stratovolcanoes.

Next time you are at the beach, make a bucket of wet, runny sand, and a bucket of harder, moist sand. Take turns pouring the sand onto one spot from each bucket, and watch how the mountain grows. Sometimes it will be lopsided if some of the sand is heavier or dribbled from off-center. Other times it will form into a perfectly even cone. But each layer makes the mountain higher, much like the way most of the Cascade volcanoes were formed. Now use a sprinkling can to rain on your stratovolcano and watch it erode. Little valleys and crevices form, just like on a real mountain.

A lava dome is a single mass of lava that surged out and formed a steep-sided mound. Cut a little hole in a piece of cardboard and stick the nozzle of a toothpaste tube up through the bottom of the hole. Squeeze gently, and watch the way it mounds up around the hole to form a dome—a lava dome. Since its eruption in 1980, Mount St. Helens has been forming a lava dome inside the crater.

A plug dome plugs up a crater left by a previous eruption. Push a tube of lipstick into the same vent, or hole, of the toothpaste lava dome you just made, then rain on it with a watering can. Little by little the softer toothpaste will be eroded, until the only thing left is the harder lipstick, the plug dome. Lassen Peak in California is a plug dome volcano.

Small, broken bits of rock and ash thrown out of a vent pile up around the hole to form a cinder cone that looks much like a pile of gravel. A cinder cone can be quite small, or it can be the size of a mountain, like Cinder Cone Mountain on the side of Lassen Peak, or Wizard Island in Crater Lake.

Did you know a volcano can erupt quietly? The Medicine Lake volcano in California is a shield volcano. These are quiet volcanoes because their lava is thin, and flows easily out of vents.

Forces inside the earth are not the only things that shaped the mountains we see today. Wind, sun, and snow also played a part by eroding the lava and rock of the volcano. Glaciers are especially good at shaping volcanoes. Glaciers are large, slow-moving masses of ice that are so heavy they are pulled downward by gravity. Over time, glaciers carve valleys and deep crevices in volcanoes.

Pacific Ocean

magma

Juan de Fuca plate

North American plate

mantle

magma

# PLATES & QUAKES

Say the word geology and some people roll their eyes and think of dirt and rocks. Big deal. Who cares about rocks? But most of us know geology is not lifeless at all—it's fascinating. Just as our bodies have interesting inner activities that aren't well-understood, so does our planet.

Geologists believe the earth has a solid core about the size of the moon, surrounded by a layer that is molten. Surrounding this molten layer is the 1,800-mile thick mantle, which is mostly solid. On top "floats" the crust, many miles thick. We live on the crust. You can compare the earth's layers to an egg: the core is the yolk, the mantle is the egg white, and the crust is the shell. Just as an eggshell can get cracks, so can the earth's crust.

The lid on a pot of soup rattles and jiggles from the pressure created by boiling liquid. Forces within the earth, where heat is concentrated, can make the earth's crust rattle and jiggle too. We call these movements earthquakes.

Magma is hot molten rock churning in chambers deep inside the earth's crust and mantle. Sometimes magma finds a crack or weak spot in the crust. The pressure is so great that the crust gives way and out spurts the magma, making a volcanic eruption.

The crust of the earth is cracked into huge sections, or plates. The plates are so thick and heavy the magma can't lift them off, just like boiling water can rattle, but not lift off, a pot lid. It can make the plates bump and grind against each other along the edges, though. Geologists call this theory of plates and their movements plate tectonics.

As the plates bump into each other, a number of things can happen. There can be earthquakes, and plates can get pushed together and form wrinkles and folds along the edges. Sometimes one plate is lighter than the other, and instead of wrinkling when they bump, the lighter one rides up over the heavy plate and covers it.

5

# A RING OF FIRE

The Cascade Mountains were formed by the movements of two tectonic plates. One is under the Pacific Ocean, and the other is under the North American continent. The heavier Pacific plate was slowly drawn under the lighter plate of North America. Then the Pacific Plate was superheated by the hot mantle of North America and its rock melted into magma. The plate on top was pushed up high above the ocean. The Cascade Mountains arose along the edge where the two plates collided and overlapped.

Tracing the Cascade Mountain Range shows us the outline of part of the Pacific plate. This plate extends from Chile to Alaska and from Japan to New Zealand. We call its outline the "Pacific Ring of Fire" because it has nearly four hundred volcanoes around its edges.

Not all the Cascade Mountains are volcanoes, but many of

Glacier Peak     Mt. Rainier     Mt. Adams

Mt. Baker     Mt. St. Helens

Mt. Hood

*Pacific Ocean*

them are. The Cascades are some of the most active volcanoes in North America. Almost all of them have shown signs of activity in the last three hundred years.

Volcanoes are said to be active, dormant, or extinct. What's the difference? Usually, "active" is used for a volcano that is erupting magma, or is almost ready to erupt. A dormant volcano is like an animal that is asleep. It is clearly alive, but is not moving about actively. But dormant volcanoes can and do enter active cycles when they may erupt. A dormant volcano is only sleeping, in other words. It could erupt again too. An extinct volcano is not expected to erupt again, and is considered dead. Of all the volcanoes in this book, only Mount Jefferson is extinct. So when you think of the Cascades, don't be fooled by the snow and ice. These are the fire mountains.

Mt. Jefferson

Three Sisters

Mt. Shasta

Lassen Peak

Crater Lake

# MOUNT RAINIER
14,411 feet (4,392 meters)

Mount Rainier is very high, but several thousand people climb to its summit every year. Climbers must be in top physical shape for the hard climb. They prepare very carefully because the climb is also dangerous. Everyone packs emergency supplies, food, extra warm clothes, and mountain-climbing equipment. Then they carry all that gear up the mountain on their backs! They really have to want to go up to be willing to do all that.

But those who have climbed Rainier say they understand what early Indians meant when they called Rainier Tahoma, "the mountain that was God." To make it to the top, risking storms or avalanches or rockfalls, is the achievement of a lifetime.

Maybe you will climb it some day. People take two or more days for the climb, often with very little time to sleep.

Mount Rainier National Park has the largest glacier system in the United States, except for Alaska. Glaciers are formed where there is snow and cold weather, and Mount Rainier has plenty of both. In some places more than fifty feet of snow falls in a single winter. One year more than ninety-three feet fell—one of the world's records.

Geologists believe Mount Rainier was once much higher than it is today, but the scraping and scouring of glaciers, as well as volcanic activity, have brought it down to its present height.

Mount Rainier is dormant, but not extinct. Geologists keep a "volcano watch" on it, constantly checking the activity deep inside. We can still see steam rising, and feel earthquakes. Do you think it will erupt again?

# MOUNT ST. HELENS

8,364 feet (2,549 meters)

The Klickitat Indians thought Mount St. Helens was a beautiful maiden, and Mount Adams and Mount Hood were her suitors. But in 1980 this lovely lady came to life, and shook the earth with terrifying power.

The eruption started with an earthquake, which shook loose the mountain's whole north side. It was the biggest avalanche ever witnessed. Over a thousand feet of earth near the top of the volcano blew to bits. Four hundred million tons of gas-filled rock shattered into dust. A pillar of ash rocketed almost fourteen miles into the air to block the sun and turn day into night. Hot volcanic gases and steam shot out sideways so fast they flattened forests seventeen miles away. The intense heat melted glaciers and snow and caused great mudflows to roar down, carrying everything in their path. The green forests that covered its sides were flattened, and clear blue Spirit Lake filled with mud and dead trees.

People two hundred miles away heard the blast. The mudflow that surged down the Toutle River at the mountain's foot buried homes and tossed huge bulldozers around as if they were small toys. Two hundred and thirty square miles of trees were blown down. Fifty-seven people were killed, as well as countless birds, fish, and animals. Rivers were choked with logs, mud, and debris, and people worked frantically for weeks to clear all the rivers and creeks so dams wouldn't break and flood even more of the countryside.

The ash cloud took fifteen days to circle the earth, and residents of Washington, Idaho, and Montana swept ash from their cars and houses. In Yakima, Washington, townspeople hauled away about 600,000 tons of ash from their homes.

In nine hours, the mountain changed from a peaceful snow-capped peak to a gray, bowl-shaped crater. Since then, Mount St. Helens has remained active. Geologists record small earthquakes coming from the mountain, and sometimes jets of ash shoot into the air. In 1982, Mount St. Helens was declared a national volcanic monument so people could see this example of nature's powerful forces. Drive around the volcano, hike to the mudflow, and look at Spirit Lake. You will see how the earth is already beginning to heal.

Mount St. Helens is quieter these days, but is definitely not sleeping. Maybe it has more surprises planned for us.

# MOUNT HOOD
### 11,235 feet (3,424 meters)

A skier whizzes down the slope and stops with a shower of snow. You can't believe your eyes. Not because of her graceful turns and daring jumps, but because it's August and you've been hiking in shorts!

Mount Hood is the highest mountain in Oregon and has eleven glaciers. It is so high that some snowfields never melt, even in summer. People from all over the world come here to ski in summer and winter.

Mount Hood is a very popular mountain because it offers so many activities. You can hike, camp, fish, climb, ski, and drive many places in the Mount Hood National Forest. Go up to Crater Rock to find fumes and vapors coming out of vents. But hold your nose—the sulphur smell can be awful. As you look at Crater Rock you can imagine the tall column going down the vent, deep into the mountain.

Other volcanic formations and debris are also easy to see on Mount Hood. The Pinnacle is a lava plug. Barrett Spur and Steel Cliff were formed by thick lava flows and mudflows. Volcanic rocks, ash, and pumice are found on the ground. Huge mudflows are easy to see. When Mount St. Helens erupted in 1980, geologists wondered if Mount Hood would do the same, since the two mountains erupted together in the

1800s. But so far, Mount Hood is still dormant.

Timberline Lodge is an interesting old building on the southeast slope of the mountain. There are enormous beams and interesting stonework, and the furniture, doors, and even the doorknobs are handmade. It is a wonderful place to warm up and rest after exploring the mountain.

An Indian legend explains the Chief's Face on Mount Hood's north side. A brave chief climbed to the summit to fight the evil spirits who lived inside. He rolled boulders into the crater, but they were thrown back out, red hot. After days of fighting, the chief looked down the valley toward his home. It was covered with ash and lava, totally destroyed. Filled with grief, he fell to the ground and was covered by lava. You can see his profile today, looking sorrowfully down the mountain.

More people climb Mount Hood than any other volcano except Mount Fuji in Japan. Climbing Mount Hood is hard work, but not dangerous in good weather. One man has climbed it almost six hundred times. A blind man, a man with no legs, and even a woman in high heels made it to the summit. She probably got the world's biggest blisters.

Mount Hood has lush evergreen forests at its base and windswept glaciers at the summit. It's a volcano inviting you to explore it.

# CRATER LAKE

Surface of the lake: 6,176 feet (1,882 meters)

Crater Lake lies inside the collapsed summit of an ancient volcano. Early Indians called this ancient volcano "the mountain that swallowed its head." One story tells that the chief of the above-world threw the top of the mountain down onto the chief of the below-world to win a great battle.

The explosion of this mountain was probably one of the most violent eruption on earth in the last six or seven thousand years. It was almost fifty times bigger than Mount St. Helens' eruption.

After the volcano blew, the summit collapsed into the hole beneath, since there was no more rock to hold it up. It made a huge, deep crater at the top which gradually filled with water from rain and melted snow. Crater Lake is 1,932 feet deep, the deepest lake in the United States. It is part of

Crater Lake National Park in Oregon. The water is intensely blue, and so clear that you can see a black and white plate 120 feet down!

Steep, many-colored cliffs rise almost two thousand feet above the lake. You can drive around the rim, hike to scenic viewpoints, or take a boat ride to Wizard Island. Wizard Island is one of two cinder cones that rise from the lake bottom. The other doesn't show above the water.

Rainbow trout, kokanee salmon, salamanders and crayfish all live in Crater Lake. Birds and mammals inhabit the area, as well as more than 570 species of ferns and plants.

Crater Lake National Park has tremendous variety and beauty. Although it has been dormant for many years, geologists know it is not extinct. Nature may be planning another fireworks display in future years. Who knows?

# MOUNT SHASTA

14,162 feet (4,316 meters)

Many people think Mount Shasta is a magic mountain. The Indians believed it was the lodge of the Chief of the Sky Spirits, who made a hole in the sky and pushed snow and ice onto the earth to form a great mountain. When smoke and fire came out, they knew the chief was at home with a fire burning inside his lodge. When he added a log, the earth shook.

Even today, some people believe that mysterious people live in the depths of the mountain. There are stories of the Lemurians, seven feet tall with extra-sensory perception, who escaped to Mount Shasta when their kingdom of Mu sank under the ocean. Other people tell of the Yaktayvians, who hollowed out caves in the mountain using the vibrations of bells and chimes. Still others believe that UFOs land in Mount

Shasta when they make a stop on earth. It must be crowded in there!

Actually, Shasta is not a single mountain at all. It is made up of as many as four volcanoes. Their lava flows overlapped so much we see one mountain instead of four, making Mount Shasta one of the biggest stratovolcanoes in the world. Shasta has snow-capped peaks, and lower slopes covered in forests.

Mount Shasta has seven glaciers, and a tiny sulphurous hot spring near the top. People enjoy skiing on the slopes, climbing to the summit, sightseeing around the base, and camping and hiking in the Shasta-Trinity National Forest.

When you visit Mount Shasta, remember to keep your eyes open for secretive people who may live inside the volcano. You just never know...

# LASSEN PEAK
10,457 feet (3,187 meters)

Geologists believe an ancient volcano named Mount Tehama once towered over northeastern California. Tehama was eroded by glaciers during the Ice Age, and about the same time an eruption through a vent on its sides created Lassen Peak.

Lassen Peak is one of the biggest plug dome volcanoes in the world. It is the only volcano besides Mount St. Helens to erupt in the lower forty-eight states in this century. Lassen Volcanic National Park has boiling, spattering, sizzling, steaming pits and pools and craters. You can hike through lovely forests and have a picnic, or pant your way to the summit.

Back when your great-great-grandparents were about your age, Lassen Peak began to erupt. It started with some explosions in the summit crater which blew out ash, mud, stones, and cinder. Then more eruptions belched out boulders and more ash. One explosion sent a column of ash more than two miles into the sky. Lassen Peak showered nearby communities with black ash while it rumbled and crashed and sent rockslides shuddering down its sides.

Lassen gave its biggest performance in May 1915. A mushroom-shaped cloud of steam and ash shot five to seven miles into the air. A giant mass of gases and steam blasted out with such force that it snapped giant trees. Lava poured out of the summit crater and spilled down the sides of the mountain. It melted the winter's snow and a giant flood roared down, carrying trees, boulders, and mud. Lassen continued to shake with smaller eruptions for the next two years.

Lassen grew quieter after 1917, but is still considered active.

Today you can explore most of the devastated area. It is still possible to see where the great blast leveled a whole forest. The Chaos Crags are large plugs, one of which collapsed and created the heaps of giant boulders called the Chaos Jumbles.

Devil's Kitchen, Bumpass' Hell, and Boiling Springs Lake are geothermal areas. These places show what happens when groundwater seeps down to the magma chambers in the earth's crust. Steam jets out from underground pools, and mud and sulphur bubble and boil in pits. Tiny spatter cones, only three to four inches across, look like miniature volcanoes.

It is fun to hike up Cinder Cone. Look into the summit craters, then turn around and see where lava flows dammed some creeks and caused Snag and Butte lakes to form.

Lassen Volcanic National Park in California will keep you busy and interested for days.

# WILDERNESS VOLCANOES

## *MOUNT ADAMS*

### 12,276 feet (3,742 meters)

If you've ever eaten a huckleberry, you'll know why families visit Mount Adams in August and September. Mount Adams has the biggest huckleberry fields in the world. Yum!

Mount Adams is the second largest volcano in the United States. It has twice the mass of Rainier, but is not quite as tall. Adams is considered dormant today.

Five thousand years ago, sulphur gases and melted water from snow and ice flowed from the summit and weakened the rocks. An enormous avalanche roared down the White Salmon River, and today you can still see big brown boulders from the summit littering the Trout Lake Valley far below the peak. In 1921 another avalanche covered almost six thousand acres with debris.

Mount Adams, in the Gifford Pinchot National Forest, is the highest mountain in our country to have ever had a fire lookout. But after working two years to build the lookout, the Forest Service abandoned it because no one could safely stay up there. Two lookout men witnessed a storm one night that blew the door right into their cabin. Electricity from lightning had melted the hinges on the door frame! Hail bounced off the ground with such force that the men said it appeared as though as much hail was going up as coming down. You can bet they were happy to get out alive.

# MOUNT BAKER
## 10,778 feet (3,285 meters)

Mount Baker is the farthest north of any of the United States' Cascade volcanoes. The Mount Baker Wilderness shares its border with Canada. Because of its northern location, Mount Baker has an annual snowfall of eighty feet...imagine eighty feet of snow! Mount Baker has so many glaciers and so much snow that it always appears covered in white. It is in the Mount Baker-Snoqualmie National Forest.

At Sherman Crater, steam vents hiss and avalanches whoosh down. Hot steam created ice caves in the glacier and the smell of sulphur is strong. Many years ago, giant mudflows poured into the valleys below.

Mount Baker is still giving off hot steam and gases, but no one knows whether it will erupt soon. Scientists watched it closely when St. Helens erupted, because the two mountains erupted within ten years of each other in 1840 and 1850. If Mount Baker does erupt, it could wipe out dams and cause disastrous flooding in nearby towns. Mount Baker is a fire mountain to keep an eye on.

# GLACIER PEAK
## 10,541 feet (3,213 meters)

Glacier Peak lies deep within the Glacier Peak Wilderness, surrounded by miles of rugged countryside and more than ninety glaciers. One of them, the Chickamin Glacier, is among the largest glaciers in the continental United States. The Glacier Peak Wilderness lies within the Mount Baker-Snoqualmie and Wenatchee national forests. It is a hiker's paradise, with more than 450 miles of trails in the remote backcountry.

Because they see so few humans, the animals often let you come quite close. Maybe you'll be lucky enough to see a mountain goat or coyote, or even a black bear. But don't get too close!

One sign that Glacier Peak is still awake are the three hot springs at its base. It is one of the most active volcanoes in the Cascade range. One eruption about twelve thousand years ago blew enough pumice and ash into the air to cover eastern Washington, Idaho, and western Montana, as well as parts of Canada.

# WILDERNESS VOLCANOES

## *MOUNT JEFFERSON*

### 10,495 feet (3,199 meters)

Lewis and Clark traveled from St. Louis, Missouri to the West Coast in 1804-6, exploring and mapping the unknown country west of the Mississippi. They named this mountain to honor President Thomas Jefferson, who sponsored their expedition. The volcano lies within the Mount Jefferson Wilderness in the Willamette National Forest. The only way to get onto the mountain is by one of the many footpaths.

Look for the wild animals that live in this wilderness, and try your hand at fishing. The high open meadows are full of wildflowers, and you can see many miles across to other Cascade volcanoes. Mount Jefferson has large glaciers which are cutting into the mountain. Maybe some of your drinking water will be melted water from a glacier.

The last time Mount Jefferson erupted was tens of thousands of years ago. Mount Jefferson is now an extinct volcano.

# THE THREE SISTERS
South Sister: 10,358 feet (3,157 meters)

Imagine a whole family of volcanic formations, with cones, craters, and buttes all clustered in one area. In the middle of these formations, three summits stick up a bit higher. These are the Three Sisters mountains, called Faith, Hope, and Charity by the early settlers. Now we know them as the North Sister, the Middle Sister, and the South Sister. They are surrounded by Little Brother, Husband, Wife, Mount Bachelor, Broken Top, Mount Washington, and others, and each one is a separate volcano.

The Three Sisters area in the Willamette and Deschutes national forests has been quiet for about three hundred to four hundred years, but this area has had more recent activity than any other part of the Cascades. Geologists believe future eruptions will occur here. The entire Three Sisters Wilderness is covered with lava, ash, and pumice.

Next time you ride the ski lift to the top of Mount Bachelor, see if you can identify all three sisters and the rest of the "family," then look farther in the distance for Mount Jefferson, Mount Hood, and even Mount Adams.

# THE MEDICINE LAKE VOLCANO & LAVA BEDS NATIONAL MONUMENT

4,000-5,700 feet (1,219-1,737 meters)

The Medicine Lake volcano is one of the largest shield volcanoes in the world. It is considered active because a fumarole near the top is always blowing steam. Lava Beds National Monument is located on its side. It is the main attraction of the Medicine Lake volcano.

At Lava Beds, wildlife enthusiasts can have a wonderful time looking for birds and animals. Bald eagles, hawks, owls, and falcons feast on the many rodents that inhabit the park, and deer browse on the shrubs.

This area was once home to the Modoc Indians, who are known for their historic fight to keep their homeland. For five months during 1872-3, a small band of fifty-three warriors held off almost a thousand U.S. soldiers! The Indians outsmarted the soldiers because they knew how to hide in the lava formations.

Lava Beds has almost two hundred lava tubes, and you can go inside many of them. A tube is created by fast-flowing lava. The outer, exposed lava cools and hardens. That hard outer layer keeps the lava inside the tube hot and liquid, so it continues to rush out until the tunnel-like tube is left empty. Exploring the tubes is fun and interesting. Some of them are coated inside with ice all year.

On the surface, you can see many other volcanic formations, such as cinder cones, spatter cones, and their lava flows. Much of the lava we see today erupted from Mammoth Crater.

# IT'S RAINING. . .AGAIN

   Winds crossing the Pacific Ocean skim across the surface, picking up moisture and carrying it to North America. It's hard to imagine wind carrying water. But think what happens when you wash a chalkboard. Wipe it with water and then it's suddenly dry again. Where did that water go? Into the air. Winds that travel across thousands of miles of ocean can absorb lots of moisture.

   Air heavy with moisture can be found almost every day in your house. Walk into the bathroom after someone has taken a shower. The moist air hangs in the room. When the moisture gets too heavy for the air to hold, it condenses and runs down the walls.

   The wind from the Pacific, heavy with moist air, arrives on the continent and suddenly slams into the Cascade Mountain Range. The only way to go is up, and the colder air of the high elevations makes the moisture condense into thick clouds. When those clouds get too heavy to hold any more water, they drop it on us, and we feel it as rain or snow.

   Down it comes, enough to fill buckets, it seems. It rains for days, and after a while you are certain the next word out of your mouth will be "quack."

   But on the other side of the Cascades, kids are playing in the sun. As a matter of fact, many people on the east side wish it would rain more often. The east side is drier because the mountains are so high that almost every bit of moisture is dropped before the wind ever makes it over the crest. The wind that finally climbs up and over is light and dry, after dumping its heavy load on you-know-who on the west slopes.

# WHO LIVES HERE?

The Cascade Mountains are swarming with living things, from tiny organisms only seen in a microscope to giant trees hundreds of feet tall.

Imagine being a marmot with a thick furry coat. Grasses are your favorite food, you can't run very fast, and your favorite winter activity is sleeping in a secret rock cave. You must live high on a mountain, where grasses grow and very few predators come. In winter, snow covers the opening to the rock cave and you hibernate, cozy as can be.

But if you are a beetle you have to live farther down the mountain, with shrubs and plants to munch on and fallen logs to live in.

What about a fox? Or a bear? Where do you think they might live?

The Cascade Mountains have very different areas, or zones, of living things. Imagine yourself on a flying carpet, surveying the range. Start at the Pacific Ocean, and swoop in on a breeze. As the Cascades loom up ahead, you see thick forests at the base. (Put up your umbrella because it's probably raining.) Peer through the dense trees and plants, and find thousands of different animals and insects who love to live there. They have many plants to eat and many places to hide in the thick vegetation.

Glide up the mountains and it gets colder. The trees are not as close together, fields of flowers bloom only in the summer, and animals and plants must be a little hardier to live up here.

Near the top of the range, only a few twisted trees and low bushes and grasses grow. They have to be really tough to survive the high winds that shake them and the deep snows that cover them each winter. Animals and insects must be able to hide under the snow and sleep most of the winter. At the summits only a few grasses thrive. If the peak has geothermal features, the heat may permit a few more plants to live, or it may be so hot and full of minerals that nothing at all lives there.

Once your flying carpet glides over the top, you see the dry, arid country spread out to the east. Because so little rain falls, the plants and animals are often quite different from the ones on the rainy side. They must be able to survive with very little water. Some animals, such as coyotes, can live on either the wet or the dry side. They are very adaptable. Other creatures, like the beaver, depend entirely on a good water supply.

Next time you are out animal-watching, notice where you are on the mountain. Think about what your animal needs to survive. What does it eat? Is there lots of that food where you are? Could the animal hide quickly if frightened? Does the animal need water nearby, or can it travel easily without much water?

Now move up the mountain, and sit quietly while you observe your surroundings. Imagine what kind of animal would like it here. It may be colder, with fewer plants to eat, but maybe the animal that lives here is smaller and doesn't eat as much. Maybe it has learned to hide in rock piles, instead of in bushes or trees. Maybe it can fly, and just visits the area you are in.

Someday sit in one spot and make a list of every living thing you see. Trees, plants, grasses, bugs, birds and animals.

Pretty amazing, isn't it?

# GLOSSARY

**Active** - A volcano that is erupting now, or shows signs of erupting in the near future.

**Ash** - Fine pieces of rock blown from a volcano.

**Cinder cone** - A pile of small, fragmented rocks piled around a vent.

**Composite volcano** - Another term for stratovolcano.

**Core** - The center of the earth, made of molten iron and nickel.

**Crater** - A bowl-shaped hollow at the top of a volcano.

**Crust** - The layer of earth we live on.

**Dormant** - A volcano that has erupted in the past, but is not in an active eruptive cycle at present.

**Earthquake** - Shaking of the earth's crust, caused by magma coming to the earth's surface, or movement of the earth's plates.

**Erode** - To wear away by the action of ice, air, or water.

**Erupt** - Burst out.

**Extinct** - Dead, not expected to erupt again.

**Fumarole** - An opening in the earth's crust which lets out steam or gases.

**Geology** - The study of the earth's rocks in order to learn about its history.

**Geothermal** - Having to do with heat from the earth's center.

**Glacier** - A mass of ice which moves very slowly.

**Lava** - Magma that has reached the earth's crust.

**Lava dome** - A mass of lava forming a steep-sided mound.

**Magma** - Molten rock below the earth's crust.

**Mantle** - Part of the earth that lies between the core and the crust. This is where magma comes from.

**Molten** - Melted into a liquid by heat.

**Plug dome** - Lava which fills or plugs a crater.

**Pumice** - Lava that has hardened around gas bubbles, so that it is frothy-looking. It is so light you can pick up a huge chunk.

**Shield volcano** - One that is broad and sloping, and has been built of thin lava flows.

**Stratovolcano** - A volcano formed of layers from different eruptions. Also called a composite volcano.

**Summit** - The highest point on a mountain.

**Vent** - An opening in the earth's surface, shaped like a tube, through which magma, gases, and other materials are erupted.

**Volcano** - Either an opening in the earth's crust through which magma erupts, or the mountain formed by the piles that are erupted.

# FOR MORE INFORMATION

For more information about your favorite Cascade volcano, please call or write the following:

**MOUNT ADAMS WILDERNESS**
Mount Adams Ranger District, 2455 Highway 141, Trout Lake, WA 98650-9046. (509) 395-2501.

**MOUNT BAKER WILDERNESS**
Mount Baker-Snoqualmie National Forest, 915 Second Avenue, Suite 442, Seattle, WA 98174. (206) 442-0170.

**CRATER LAKE NATIONAL PARK**
Crater Lake National Park, P.O. Box 7, Crater Lake, OR 97604. (503) 594-2211.

**GLACIER PEAK WILDERNESS**
Mount Baker-Snoqualmie National Forest, 915 Second Avenue, Suite 442, Seattle, WA 98174. (206) 442-0170.

**MOUNT HOOD**
Mount Hood National Forest, 2955 Northwest Division, Gresham, OR 97030. (503) 666-0771.

**MOUNT JEFFERSON**
Willamette National Forest, Blue River Ranger District, Blue River, OR 97413. (503) 822-3317.

**LASSEN VOLCANIC NATIONAL PARK**
Lassen Volcanic National Park, P.O. Box 100, Mineral, CA 96063-0100. (916) 595-4444.

**LAVA BEDS NATIONAL MONUMENT**
Lava Beds National Monument, P.O. Box 867, Tulelake, CA 96134. (916) 667-2282.

**MOUNT RAINIER NATIONAL PARK**
Mount Rainier National Park, Tahoma Woods Star Route, Ashford, WA 98304. (206) 569-2211.

**MOUNT ST. HELENS NATIONAL VOLCANIC MONUMENT**
Mount St. Helens Visitor Center, 3029 Spirit Lake Highway, Castle Rock, WA 98611. (206) 274-6644.

**MOUNT SHASTA**
Shasta-Trinity National Forest, 2400 Washington Avenue, Redding, CA 96001. (916) 246-5222.

**THREE SISTERS WILDERNESS**
Willamette National Forest, Blue River Ranger District, P.O. Box 199, Blue River, OR 97413. (503) 822-3317.

# CONCLUSION

The Cascade volcanoes remind us that nature is never asleep. It's easy to understand why ancient peoples believed that volcanoes were living beings, sometimes noisy and dangerous, other times peaceful and kindly.

Forces deep within the earth can both create life and destroy it. Although most of the Cascades have not erupted for many years, remember that they are completely beyond the control of human beings. They are the teachers, and we can only watch and learn from them.

## Interpreting the Great Outdoors

Nature's wonders, such as the volcanos of the Pacific Northwest, are certainly remarkable, but unfortunately many people—especially young people—know little about them. That's one reason Falcon Press has launched this series of books called Interpreting the Great Outdoors.

Natural phenomena almost always have interesting and exciting stories behind them, stories too good to leave to scientists and naturalists. With this series of books, we hope to tell why, when, where, and how the wonders of nature came to be. We want to help satisfy the natural curiosity of our young readers.

Look for other books in Falcon Press' Interpreting the Great Outdoors series. They include *The Tree Giants: the story of the redwoods, the world's largest trees;* and *California Wildflowers: a children's guide to the state's most common flowers.*

To obtain extra copies of this book or others in the Interpreting the Great Outdoors series, write to Falcon Press, P.O. Box 1718, Helena, MT 59624. Or call toll-free 1-800-582-BOOK. Falcon Press publishes and distributes a wide variety of books and calendars, so ask for our free catalog.